ABHIVYAKTI

AN ANTHOLOGY OF POEMS AND QUOTES

PRATIBHA KUMARI SINGH

To …

the lord

who guides

every moment

and

on every path

Contents

Contents

Acknowledgements

Indebtedness, first and foremost to my family: Guru, my husband from Shiv Nagari Kashi, who always encourages me to discover my true self; Anvay, the elder one, a 15 years lad, a gadget freak whose passion and speed gives me a challenge to move out of my comfort zone and test my love for writing and polishing this craft every now and then; younger one Anvit, four and a half years of age whose naughtiness echoes in the pages; and loving Maa whose calm presence always assures completion of work that I undertake.

My heartfelt gratitute to amazing friends and colleagues at SRM University Sikkim for their literary acumen and penmanship that catalyzed this verse writing process. My mentors, freinds and collegaues at Ansal University with whom I have had one of the most cherishing time and their love and blessings still nourish my individual quest.

School and college friends, I am thankful to each one of them, without their presence my existence is questionable. I thank to each one of them, without their contribution on every day basis, I wouldn't have composed and lived a life of happiness and fulfillment that I am experiencing and living at the moment.

Scholarly students, whose sharp intellect and creative zeal keep honing the edges of my teaching and writing profession, ensuring momentum of academic rigour, I therefore bow to each one of them.

Sapna Mangala, Author of *Zoya a Girl Full of Life* and Riddhi Mangala for their encouraging words and suggesting Notion Press to get this anthology published. Pradyumn Singh Jadon, my brother for his guidance and vision.

Entire Team at Notion Press desrves speacial mention and indebtedness to each one of them for encourging authors and writers at every step through their continousguidance.

Image credits are due to Canva app; Sketches and Matuh.

Last but not the least, my teachers, mentors, trainers, academicians, professionals, poets and writers whom I read and have had the opportunity to interact and work with, without their blessings, this work wouldn't have been possible.

Preface

When you have flair and taste for words, their melody and sound touch your soul. It is difficult to resist yourself from admiring the voices and craft of other poets and writers. This happened with me. I picked up two works : *Monk on a Hill* by Guru T. Ladakhi and *Kora* by Tenzin Tsundue, fourteenth edition from Rachana Bookhouse, Gangtok, Sikkim. This poetic work is thus, purely inspired by these poets. Their voices resonated with my inner voice and an inner compulsion prompted me to compose these verses. They have their narratives to unveil though their poems, I have my stories and lore to sing through my verses. This becomes my first attempt at publishing poetry thus, and I feel humbled and elated at the same time to read what I wrote until they got printed on the pages.

This anthology reflects those subjects and ideas that have personally shaped me and intrigued me in my journey till now, they, therefore make five sections of the book: self; home; work; nature and meditation; in which this book has been categorized. The mood and tone are inquisitive and affirmative-- something that reflect my authentic way of being.

My writing journey as a blogger completes seven years. All my blog posts have been mirror of my personal journey. This book is also not an exception to this, however, the purpose is to take you along in a journey and enable you to discover the 'poetic you' through not only reading, but also penning down your personal reflections at the end of each section. A sense of elation is natural, along with gaining a deeper sense of satisfaction at each verse completion-I thus promise to each one of you.

With me, try these...doodle the words, scribble the bizarre ideas, become maverick in perceiving the world, forget commas and full stops and let the lyric of your inner soul sing the elegy or the ode, compose an epic or a poetic prose and then revise, that comma (,) or a missing full stop (.). Whatever, it does, allow your mind, heart and soul to pour your being into it.

Wishing you all happy reading and writing with *Abhivyakti* !!

SELF

This forms the first section of this anthology of collection. This section inquires this inquisitiveness to know who am I. This thirst to know what makes me the 'way I am' becomes very intense at a time wherein we experience an inner urge to probe deeper and deeper and become aware of the inner dimensions of this search-within and in the world outside both manifesting the answers that we seek. The questions of identity, aim, purpose, individualism, roles, society and many more that hook us… we try to understand them.

In the poems, hence, I have tried to weave the notions and ideas of self around personal experience and urge each one of you to dig and probe what makes you-you. The more you know, the better you shall feel and be at peace with your authentic self of who you are in complete acceptance of the way you are and then progressing on your evolutionary journey.

1. Self

"When I close my eyes, then also I search

Even when words do not reach me, then also I listen..."

2. QUEST

Unending, relentless it is
In search I am
No guilt
No shame
I am
Who I am
With them
With the self
Proud of my presence
In the way I am
Acceptance of the infliction and then the blames
What I did and what I didn't
Conscious or unconscious of those deeds
That make me
Who I am
The way I am
In the shops
In the markets
On the roads
While making my debits
At the cafes

While eating the puddings
Giving the credits
Making the praises
In search of the truth I am
In quest
Is still …
I am?

3. ASK

Questions, my bosom friends, always sat by my side
They were more in numbers than the full stops
Sign of exclamations found place because I always wondered
Yet …the questions always led me to look for the next answers:
What's next?
What's today?
Why this?
Why not that?
Here or there?
Where it would be the best?
If here, then how?
If how, then when?
If when, then where?
If where, then when again?
You can too…
Try this out
Ask and then ask again
Enquire and Question
You will get an answer
Keep on asking
Until you get 'the' answer
Or many answers

Depending on type of question that you ask
Giving you the clarity
Will you?
I don't know about you
I know…I will continue to
Ask

4. WHO AM I?

Who makes me the way I am…
The society I live in?
My parents ?
My environment ?
My country, my nation?
My religion or faith?
My friends ?
My psyche?
My education?
Or the time of births that I have taken?
Why I am the way I am
Sometimes or most of the times…
I wonder
I change
My values also I consciously now make an attempt
To change
I don't know how
Like Domino's effect
Suddenly on one day I realize
I have changed completely
From what I was

To a new self that I am
Whom I like the more
That I myself don't know
All I know is
I am another self of who I was or used to be
Who or what makes me this 'I'
'I' or something that is part of me
Or something external
I know, yet I don't know
I witness thus
Because they told
To enquire and continue to probe
Until I realize
Who I am.

5. LESSONS ON MY WAY

I learned the lessons on my way
Of the failures and success
Of what works and what doesn't
Of what is important and significant
Of what is real and what transcendence
I learned the lessons on my way
I learnt …
Repeat what you know and gain the mastery
Continue the work and understand the appropriateness, relevance and simplicity
Fear not of the outcome, because it is in the mind
It is the fruit of the Karmic account, so work ceaselessly to make it undermine
Focus on what is important to achieve what you desire in life
A set goal of Arjuna is important to be materialized
Like him, the scion of the Bharata
I know of what is yet to be known
Of knowing my past, present and futuristic ways
Because I am embarked on the unknown ways
Thus

I realized the reality of my limitedness
I also realized the value of my limitlessness
Ultimately
I offer all fruits of action to him
To Madhav --my Kanha
With him, through him...
I learned the lessons on my way
And proudly
I am still learning the lessons on my way

6. SELF

Unveiling every moment
Unseen, unknown
Trance bliss
In togetherness we see
Precious, serene
These moments make us feel
The self that witness everything the way it is
New or old
Ennui amidst thrill
How it will come, not known
Like the flute
Symphony
Music of the moment
We know how to play music of life
Our passions, ambitions, dreams
Our family, our home, our words
Something like...
Floccinaucinihilipilification
Stange and infinite
They all are part of life
They all give meaning

They all define the self
And yet
None of these is
What we call and know
What we define and know
The known and the unknown
The explorer and the explored
The Self…

When I reach to the zilch

I realize my true self

That assures every second

That I am complete

HOME

Once in *Fundamentals of Public Speaking* class I had asked from Pooja, a studemt, what she would want to become after her graduation, she had answered-a house wife. This was a surprise for me then. Now, after being a homemaker and a mom, I realize and understand how home makes me feel and live the life that I dream and yearn to live.

For, home is a dwelling place. A place where we live our lives. Life of dreams and ambitions, family and completion.

What makes a home? What makes us feel at home? These are the questions that I have tried to answer through my personal understanding and everyday experience of being a home maker in the following poems.

Peace, truth, tranquility, happiness and all such emotions we experience being at home, besides these, we do feel sad, adrift, and alone, being at our home. This section therefore, takes us to travel within, enabling us to find newer meanings and revelations about our abode and perceive it new ways. Let's re-define our homes.

Can we?

7. Home

My abode of rest and work

Where I am the way I am

8. MY ANGEL

My little angel demands attention
He orders for pizza and alloo mimmi
Likes to eat he, and clearly blabbers about his needs
I give him attention, yet feel bereft of it
He loves food, everyday purchase of toys with Papa
Watching his favorite Vlad and Nikki
Toys and dumptruck
Making all of us dumbstruck
A car and a motor truck
Bat he holds with basket ball
In one hand ice cream and other one he demands Pasta with football
Stubborn and cranky, shouts out loud for everything
Lets go and play Mamma he would speak in a softer tone
When angry, he would change his tone and demeanor
He asks me to hold him and then do
Round and round and round and round
Round and round and round and rounds
Mamma *fir se*...once again, he cajoles
Round and round and round and round
Round and round and rounds and rounds

The moments pass by and the cosmos blurs
I holding him and we are still engrossed
In round and round and round and round
Again I cwtch him and we still engrossed
In Round and round and round and rounds

9. CONNOISSEURS

There is this hunger
That comes and knocks everyday
I have to abide and listen to her
The only way to pacify her
Is by cooking
I cook
I am not that good
I am learning
They love
My family
All members
They are connoisseur and critics of high class
A pinch of a salt and a tea spoon of turmeric
In just the right proportion
Is their precision
Accuracy all dishes must have
Deliciousness with delicacy
Taste must not be compromised at any cost
Aroma should convey beforehand--if you cooked well
Passion and nutrition are intermixed
Platter and cusine are explored in

Gourmet they are
Trust me, when I unveil
My family members are...
The connoisseurs of high class

10. CLEANING

Artifacts and objects
When neglected in home
For a long time -remain unattended
When time allows
A piece of cloth taken
Soaked in solution
We clean a holder, stand or a vase
We could see the lines of dirt stick
Embraced and holding they remain to each other
Looks as if in perfect unison
The object and the dirt
In my home they are
Now they are cleaned
Spic and span they are
They reflect a part of who I am
Shine forth my consciousness
Now I understand
When they say:
'Keep polishing the mirror'
Why it is so important
Their presence in my home

For home is the seat of cleaning
Cleaning of my conscience
At home I am
In the process of cleaning I am

11. FAMILY AND HOME

Decor of every nook and corner
Scribble and scratches on the wall
A nail here and a there
To put up painting on the wall
Curtains on the window
Wind chimes besides the wooden drawer
Keeping the piles of papers and books on shelves
There are a myriad of posters and stickers that stand tall
The broom and the mop
The wiper and the 10x lizol
Soaps and tooth-paste with brushes in abundances
Skates, school shoes and down shoes
Mechanic set for car design
Kept amidst a guitar
The veggies in the kitchen
Smile with drums of rice and flour
Chilies and coriander rest in basket of fruits
A lighter, a pair of tongs, mustard oil can
All enjoy with ladle in the vessel pool
Their presence make us feel at home

We are at home
With live with people whom we call
Maa & Paa
Daughters and sons
Husband and wife
They make our family
Family--that completes our home
Home…then what is for you?
Things or people?
Feelings or emotions?
Safety or protection?
Bonding or promises?
Arguments or agreements?
Solitude or togetherness?
None of these?
Or all of these?
With family once again
I decorate every nook and corner of my home

12. HOME COMING

When children rush to home
From school in a state of frenzy
They all look elated
Happiness echoes in their run
In their shouts they express
Freedom, fearlessness
How it will come to us
Not known to me
Like the flute
Symphony
Music of the moment
I am learning
How to play music of life
With my passions, ambitions and dreams
They all give me life
Every moment to me is
Like Home Coming
Like children I am becoming
Relishing every moment of my home coming

All come for a reason in my life

To know the reason is to serve my purpose

WORK

I have family and friends whom I would define or call 'Karmayogis'. They believe in action and work. They are driven by personal goals and societal ambitions. Individuals yearning to find fulfillment in the individual pursuit that they all are engaged in.

Work is a medium and then an end also to realize their true self. In their individual pursuit, they understand the very nature of their existence and also find inner zeal and zest on everyday basis on whatever work they like and are framed in. In fact, every profession is result of this action orientation. Therefore, it is Important for each one of us to take action, work, apply will and thoughts in accomplishment of our aims and goals. I am working because ...

WORK IS WORSHIP

13. Work

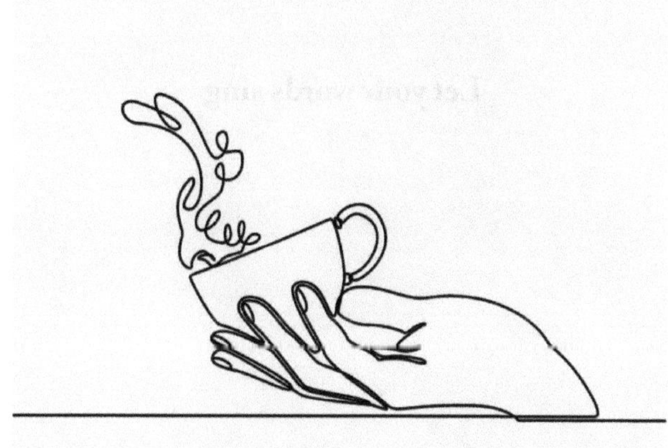

Work in silence

Work with silence

Let your actions speak

Let your words sing

14. TEST AND TRIAL

I read them
Voluminously and voraciously
I liked them-the prose and poems
They were given in the syllabus
When I was young in school and college
We analyzed
We critically evaluated them
They brought meaning and revelation when the teacher taught
Now
I am a teacher
I write them
In a state of contemplation and pondering
Or following the stream of consciousness
I try to capture the moment
Want to see how 'they' wrote
Because I feel myself one of them
When they wrote
"willing suspension of disbelief"
"or emotions recollected in tranquility"
I want to examine

What works for me
Knowledge of the theory
Or the practice
Word power
Or the conscious choice
I want to test
And try
What works and what doesn't

15. COMMA

Physics, Chemistry, Biology
Zoology, History, Sociology
Psychology, Food, Technology
Travel, Tourism and Hospitality
Mathematics with Kitchen live
Subjects, courses infinite
Core, electives
Specializations, professionalism
A story and its intriguing plot
Theme following the context
My struggle and identity quest
Is there any, I ask?
You tube videos, likes on Facebook
Twitter, tumbler and blogs
Like untaught Marketing and taught Rhetoric
By
the Greeks
and
The Romans
I feel to grab and learn all
In this life time

Is it possible?
I don't know
If I would come across
Any stop…
Because fields, subjects
Each for me
Turns into a comma soon
I don't know this
If I would
Come across
When and where
To a full stop

16. INTENTIONS

At the beginning of any task or work
Set intentions of what do you want
The clarity will bring results
Nuggets of wisdom on the path
A simple aim of completion
Or ambitious goal of gaining accomplishments
Whatever you intend
It shall be manifested
Achieving purity
Or churning of the self
Once you know what you want
The focus has to be on the next step
When the impediments block the road
The bottle neck freeze the thought process
Find the mentor and the guide
Read or write to find the clues
Note them, record them and then move on
Either on the untrodden or the trodden one
Remember…
You just need to decide
Your intentions

17. STEPS

One at a time
Just like when we write
A word, a phrase and then a sentence
One at a time
A step at a time
Overlap may occur to make it real
Yet, we know, and now have realized
Only one at a time
Step that we can take
Backward or forward that is a choice
Yet with the goal in the mind
Take one step at a time
Of a dance or a walk
Of a manuscript or a deposit
Synchronized with your fellow-travellers
Or independently idealized
Everything you have to decide
Different for each one of us
Though are the steps
Yet the same they are
For continuously we need to take them

After some time
Our consciousness become incisive
Penetrating and discriminating with practice
We take our steps
Then also …
One at a time
One at a time
One at a time

18. WORK

From making my tea
To writing words
From arranging the desk
To cleaning the tabs
From stacking the files
To reading the alphabets
From picking up the toys
To keeping them in the bag
From eating the meal
To relishing every morsel
From arranging the clothes
To dressing-up my self
From reading the books
To making perpendiculars
From walking on the road
To being at the home
From marking the calender
To counting each breath
From washing the clothes
To ironing them on the board
From sweeping the floor

To mopping up the floor
From frying in the pan
To serving in the bowl
From typing the words
To taking a pause
I am in 'Work'
Work that is in progress
In that mode of work
Like he says - Sadhguru
I am...
'In motion with stillness'

Learning is important, so is unlearning

Choose wisely, know their difference

NATURE

Nature is manifestation of God's presence in our lives. We are dependent for our survival on it. Its vastness and infinity makes us question the very existence of our being. We are one of the species on this earth, on this planet. We are all evolving like the other species.

Being human makes us thus, work consciously on the virtues that nurture blooming of our true infinite potential and realize our true self that can be attained by being in the company of nature and getting inspiration from it.

My Papa and Maa both loved nature. Being a student of literature allowed me to delve into the verses of Wordsworth, Keats, Shelly, Hopkins, Kalidas, Tagore, Torulata Dutt, Mahadevi Verma, Ram Dhari Singh Dinakr, Maithali Sharan Gupt to name a few. These poets were deeply moved by the beauties and bounties of nature; mountains, rains, birds and valleys, rivers and tree casuarina that touched me and all those who love literature and poetry.

Through these poems, therefore, I invite you all once again to experience the vastness and divinity of nature. Take a nature walk or observe a flower! Just that and nothing else is required…to just 'Be.'

19. Nature

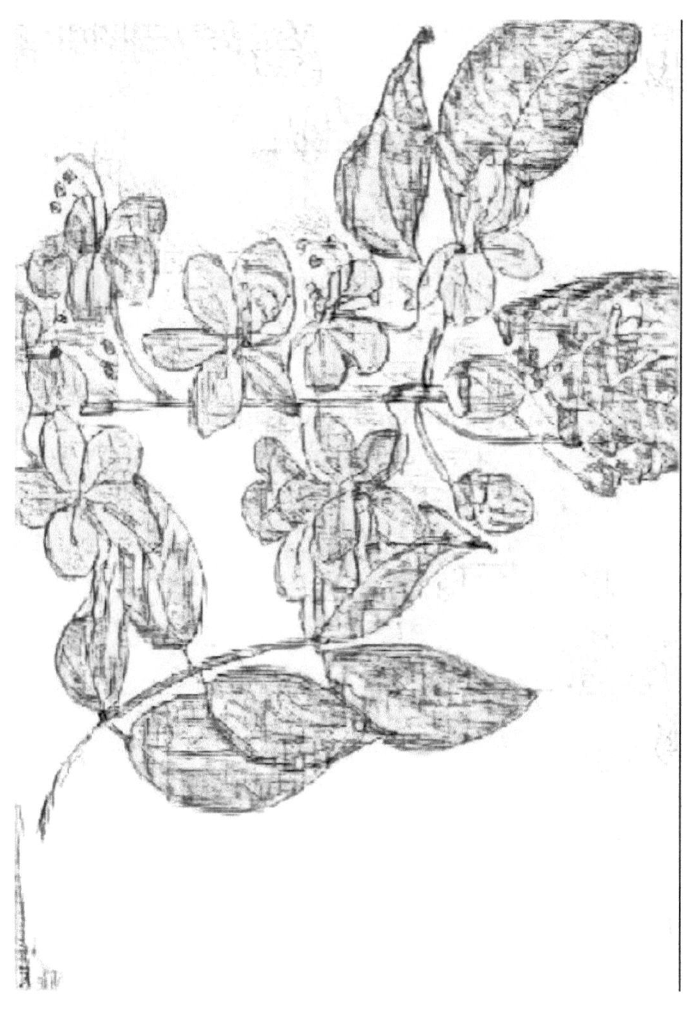

I am fragrance ...

I am colours ...

I am God's message

I am nature

20. THERE AND HERE

From the land of dessert storm
I am now residing at a place of hail storm
Arravali mountains protect there and embrace the valley
Here, Tista flows to give life to floral beauties and bounties
There, the temperature reaches to 45 Degree Celcius
Here, in winters it is minus, lowest recorded -10 Degree Celcius
Scorching heat and burning Sun is life there
Spine chilling cold here, with showers of rains makes life here
I grew up there playing and reading
Growing here I am, writing and meditating

21. PEACE

Out of the window
When I see
All I see are
Trees with green leaves
They move gently and softly with breeze
Breeze that allows the leaves to breathe
When they breathe
We too breathe
And then a sudden gush of life's energy
They call it "chi"
We feel…
This feeling by gentle breeze inspires
Inspiration that gives life to work
Work that aligns with our 'inner nature'
This inner nature feels tired and fatigued
Fatigued after the day's chores
Exhausted and drained to the core
Yet these leaves and breeze inspire
Inspire to be gentle and calm
With calmness focus and sit
Sit to work on the mission and goal
Goal that gives sense of purpose and direction
Accomplish it without thinking of the result

Like the tree with its fruits
And then feel at peace.
It is nature that gives solace
With them here, I am at peace!

22. RAIN-TODAY

Rain is loud today
I am unable to listen to anyone
It is outlandish
Very intense and severe
I have to keep calm
The mountains are invisible
So are the clouds unseen
Roads are drenched completely
So has everything
No one is visible to me
From my window
On the other side...life is moving on intensely
What I need to do is just keep silence
And observe when it stops
It is blissful to associate with rain
When you loose a part of yourself
Merge with the sounds of rains
You know not where you are
You become rain in rains

23. I LOOK UP TO YOU

Every time I look for inspiration
I look up to you …
Every time I feel burnt out
I look up to you…
Every time there is crisis
I look up to you …
Every time there is inner struggle
I look up to you …
Every time there is problem to solve
I look up to you…
Every time there is something to write
I look up to you…
Every time there is work to do
I look up to you…
Every time you show your eternity
I pigmy, surrender to your cosmic immensity
In my fulfillment of nothingness
I look up to you...

24. NATURE: VAST AND INFINITE

They all, the modernists and romanticists
Worshiped nature
I too follow them
Being a Pantheist now
For it is infinite and serene
Bound and magnificently rich
Unfathomable and unreachable
Forests-lush-green-and-wildly-intimate
Lands boundless spread across horizons
Sky like a covering night and days in different shades
Beautiful and infinite
Lines and dots they all connect
To this earth
To this globe
To the planets galore
To the sun and the moons
To the starts that shine bright at night
To the million galaxies I bow
To the Nature that is vast and infinte

I am the leaf and the tree

I am the fruit and the seed

I am everything, yet nothing

Is this my journey?

MEDITATION

Dhayana or Meditation is a spiritual practice. This practice aims to attain inexplicable peace and bliss within. Each one of us, without exception, through every pursuit, consciously or unconsciously strive to attain that state in a myriad of ways. Siddhartha, the Gautama propounded the balanced way to meditate on the inner self and that is the way to reach to Nirvana-Enlightenment. We all are on that way, with our individual choices to attain that Boddhisattva. The poems in this section are a reflection of the personal understanding of the very nature of meditation, through readings, reflections and talks and I believe it shall resonate with each one of you.

25. Meditation

I have all the answers known to me

Still I ask, because they make me who am
I

26. 'THOU ART THAT'

Thou art that
I was told
I was taught
I contemplated and then
My inflated ego worked
Sometimes...
Not all the times
I can't claim
It is a vikar, the scriptures proclaim
A vice or a folly that one must become aware of
I am aware of that
That is my vikar- the folly to work upon
Yet I know, it is a part of me
It makes me who I am
The way I am
The way I work and exhibit my self
And then when the antithesis to this says
'Thou art that'
The complete-the one
Then how does it matter
What *vikars* I have
I am one with them
In complete acceptance of my self

Conscious of my err and progress
Path trodden and yet to to be travelled
Let me be with my self
For I love and accept the way I am
One I am-with my inflated self
In complete acceptance of
Thou Art That

27. SAT-CHIT-ANANDA

Without exception you and me
We both in togetherness
Want to be happy and sail through the times
Time that is immemorial
That define and determine change
With that change you and me are born again
To realize our true self
Through every pursuit that we undertake
In ambiguity and clarity
Whenever we seek our shelter
We experience this
Truth is one : sat
This propels us to consciousness
A level of purity: chit
A state of consciousness
Because of cause and effect
Of practice incessent
Continously working on a equation
A connect with the self and the Supra
We reach to that state
We call it Ananda-Pure Bliss
I know you have experienced it

Just stay there
With me
And with them
Forever !

28. Reflections On...

I listen to their sounds
Listening is dear to me
In silence
I reflect
Shravan-manan-niridhayasana
They say, the Gurus
They give Sutras
I practice
I don't know how intensely
Yet I do practice and follow
The steps are simple
1, 2 and 3
First : Listen
Second : Reflect
Third : Practice
And then
Repeat this…
This cycle
of
Shravan-manan-niridhayasana

29. SHUNAYA

Circle and a line
Geometry and algebra
Aligned they both must be
1, 2, 3, 4 and 5
I feared the numbers and tables when a child
Grown up now I am in numbers
Age approximately now-- 39
Inverse them, when I they result into 93
Add one, difference of a decade they make
In 10 years world change
So will I
Beyond tables and numbers
Greater 'than' and smaller 'then'
Polynomials and natural numbers
I shall merge into
Shunaya

30. MEDITATION

Take a breath
Heave in silence
Sit in lotus posture
And close your eyes
Smile
Observe
Meditate on a name
A point
A candle
Or
Its flame
Focus
Watch the mind
Wandering thoughts
Like clouds
Just witness
Allow them to pass
The thoughts
They are temporary
Nothing is permanent
Do not associate
Do not follow
Just observe in the detached way

For a minute
Or if you want, for some more time
If you want, set the clock for sometime
And then just …
Focus on the breath
Inhale and exhale
Count them if you want
That's how we begin to meditate
Notice the gentle rise and fall
Of the breath and of the muscles
Of the body and where you are
In the moment
Just stay there
In oneness
In meditation

Surrender humbly all I to him…

And my way unveils cosmically

Epilogue

There is an 'unsung' and 'unborn' poet within each one of us. These poems are the essence of that eternal self that is poetic in nature.

Ideally before writing this epilogue, there should have been a prologue detailing how these poems should be approached. However, consciously I choose not to do so--reasons obvious. For I wanted a self directed reading by each one of you. Each one of us is at a level of consciousness and stage that requires some moments of reflection and realization of merging into that. Trance, bliss, eureka all are found in that moment itself. There is no expectation from you, rather I want you to travel within …with reading, re-reading of each composition. When you come across 'a word' or 'a clause' or 'a phase' or a moment that cragfast to you, I want you to be deeply absorbed into that moment and then stay there for some time. Experience how it had felt and how it feels now in present. And if a part of your self propels and wants you to compose or scribble something then do that because I invite you in this journey of self discovery through writing words.

Words have power. Words have energy. Words care. Words harness bonding. The more we know and understand, the closer we come to our true self. More than anyone else, it is 'we' who need our maximum attention and care and therefore, it is important that we focus on transformation within. In most of the poems, there is 'I' and use of first person expression, and that is simply to express what

I feel and the way I perceive the world. My 'I' is "aham" and very existence of who I am. No one is like me and I am unlike others and therefore, to celebrate this individualism, I invite you to write and compose when time allows and feelings overpower.

In such a moment then ...you feel a dire urge to express and in another moment you just empty yourself that is how it is and when you look back, you can identify a part of you and its growth in the journey of not only knowing the truth rather experiencing it also. It is *Abhivyakti.*

Abhivyakti means self expression and in whatever we do, we are always expressing ourselves, so just compose and let a part of your self find expression through words...

9 798887 496207

Printed by Libri Plureos GmbH in Hamburg,
Germany